Contents

How can I help my child become a reader?

An exciting journey

Becoming a reader is one of the most demanding and exciting stages in your child's life.

A whole world opens up as they start to make sense of letters and sounds. From seeing marks on a page to understanding that these marks have meaning, from recognising letters to reading simple words, and then becoming a fluent and confident reader – this is an incredible journey!

Helping your child become a reader means you can go on this journey together. All children learn in different ways and at different speeds, but through everyday simple and fun activities you can be an amazing resource for encouraging and developing their skills.

Children make their first discoveries about reading and writing at home. They see you relaxing with books, magazines or the paper. They see the things you do every day – writing a shopping list, scribbling a date on the calendar, following a recipe, checking the TV guide, sending a text, ordering from a catalogue or a website. You are demonstrating how vital, useful and enjoyable reading and writing are to our lives.

This guide from Letterland is designed to help you join and support your child on their journey into reading and writing. It will introduce you to different stages of literacy – speaking and listening, letter shapes and sounds, making words and reading to learn – and give you practical ideas for things you can do easily and every day to help develop your child's reading and writing skills. It also gives you activities and games that you can download, and places you can go for more help.

The practical tips generally refer to children from around 2-7 years old (or above for English language learners).

However, there aren't any references to age in this guide. This is because children develop at different speeds – a group of five year-olds will all be at very different stages in their literacy development.

On the final pages you will meet the Letterland characters – friendly people and animals who really help children learn and remember letter shapes and sounds.

On page 31 you will find information on common problems that children might experience while learning to read and write, and answers to questions that parents and carers often ask.

Introduction to Letterland

Do you remember how you learned to read and write as a child? You probably don't. However you were taught, your child's school is likely to be teaching in a different way now and using different resources. But the good news is that there are many ways in which you can support, encourage and enthuse your child throughout the whole learning process – before school, when they start to read and beyond into full fluency.

Most schools now use phonics-based teaching in the early days of reading and writing. This means children are taught to recognise letter sounds, segment them (say their sounds separately) and then blend them to make whole words. But the English language is complex and contradictory – there are only 26 letters, but 44 speech sounds. So some letters have to represent several sounds (for example, **chat**, **school**, **cat**, **hat**,) and, worse still, identical sounds may be represented by quite different letters (for example, **wait**, **late**, **way**, **they**, **eight**). The result is lots of rules and broken rules!

To explain all the complexities and contradictions to a child beginning to read and write, in language they understand, is a huge challenge. This is where Letterland comes in.

Letterland is an imaginary place full of bright and friendly letter characters who capture children's imaginations and help them make sense of letters and the sounds they make, separately and when they meet and make a new sound in a word.

Hi! I'm Harry Hat Man. I hate noise, so I whisper my sound in words like this: 'hhh...'

Rather than learning rules, children learn little stories about Annie Apple, Harry Hat Man, Clever Cat and others. These stories translate the dry rules into child-friendly information which they actually enjoy remembering.

As well as helping children to link specific sounds with each letter, the characters explain why letters combine to make new sounds like **sh**, **ch**, **ar**, **er**, **ow**, **oi**, **ea**, **igh**. This story logic makes the phonic facts stick, providing the precious keys that open the doors to literacy.

Whenever Sammy Snake starts to hiss behind Harry Hat Man, the Hat Man turns back and says 'sh!' because he hates noise.

The characters also help with letter formation as they fit within the letter and follow its shape. To describe where to start and finish a letter you simply describe the movement around a character. And talking about the character as you describe its formation also helps reinforce the letter sound.

An added bonus is that the characters and stories entertain as they teach, turning this new world of print into a friendly and fun place to be.

Learning to read and write is like learning to unlock a code. It's easy if you have the key! With Letterland you and your child can enjoy unlocking the door to literacy together.

Lyn Wendon – **originator of Letterland**

⬇ Free downloads & resources

1. Introduction to Letterland
Find out how Letterland makes learning to read & write fun and simple to remember.
www.letterland.com/parent-guide

Speaking and listening

Talking matters

Talking to your child and responding to the sounds they make – starting even before they can say actual words – gets their ears listening and brain alerted to you and to their surroundings, and develops their ability to talk too. Later on, these early language skills will carry over into reading and writing. All those words you use to speak and read to them will help to widen their vocabulary, develop their verbal confidence and provide a great foundation for learning to read and write. So talking matters!

Taking part in conversations with you, listening to stories, thinking with you about the events and ideas in stories and in daily life, asking and answering questions, singing songs together – all these things are a very valuable part of developing your child's ability to listen, think, and speak confidently, both at home and away from home.

Sharing all sorts of books is a wonderful added bonus! In the beginning you will be helping your child to discover how books work – the correct way round to hold them, that they have a beginning and an end, that their pages turn one at a time, and that there is a reading direction.

More importantly, you will be helping your child to discover that reading is fun and enjoyable and that books can take you places! You will be getting your child used to hearing the language of stories, and the wide range of interesting words in them.

Books also give you a rich way to communicate with your child, for you to explore together the remarkable range of experiences that books hold, and to talk about them while you are sitting cosily together. They give your child a time, too, to express their own thoughts and emotions while they have your undivided attention. These times are so valuable in preparing your child to become a good communicator with a wide vocabulary that will be useful throughout daily life.

Consider this: Research has shown that children with the widest vocabularies become the most successful in school and even on into their adult lives. Why? Because they have become skilled communicators. Language skills open doors..

So reading together with your child combines the benefits of talking, listening, storytelling and thinking – all helping to build the foundation for your child's thriving language development.

Once children are reading independently, they will probably still want you to read stories to them, because you have made it into a special time which you have both enjoyed together. If so, you will have already set them on an upward path, so congratulations!

Tips and Activities

✓ **Too early?** It is never too early to start reading to your child. Small babies love looking at bright pictures and hearing your voice. Ideally begin while they are just babies on your lap! Your warm attention, your flow of words, and your finger pointing to things in the pictures, these are all helping to form their thinking brains.

✓ **Too late?** A child is never too old to want a story. Children enjoy being read to even when they can read fluently. Involve other family members, and make reading storybooks part of your family life style. It will pay huge dividends when it turns your child into a reader for life.

Daily? Try to read to or with your child every day, even if it's just for ten minutes. However, if your child is too tired or not in the right mood to listen to a story, don't put them off by insisting on doing it just then. Simply find another time.

Best timing? There is no 'best' time or place to read with your child. Reading stories at bedtime is a good way for your child to relax and wind down. You can also snatch little moments any time to read notices in a waiting room, adverts on a bus, books on a park bench, cereal packets in the supermarket, etc.

Visit your local library. It is free to join, and many of them run interesting events for younger children such as storytelling, rhyme time, and story-related arts and crafts events.

Pictures and words. Look at lots of picture books, read stories and rhymes and sing songs together. Borrow books, buy books as presents, and swap books with friends so you always have something interesting to read in the house.

Don't just read. You don't need to read every word at first. You could just enjoy the pictures, talk about them, and work out together what is happening in them. Adjust the wording to suit your child's level of understanding. Another time enjoy the full story.

Check first. Read through a new book before you share it so you are ready to use lots of expression, or funny voices to add interest and make your child laugh.

Rereading. Be willing to reread favourite books many times. You could swap roles sometimes, too. Have your child pretend to be the grown-up and 'read' some of that familiar book to you, or to just talk to you about what's happening in the pictures.

Ooops! Make deliberate mistakes when reading a very familiar story or singing a nursery rhyme. You could make this into a game, so your child is on the alert to catch you out. Then they can have the fun of correcting you.

Finger pointing. Point to words in the story from time to time to draw your child's attention to particular words, where they begin and end, and how the story is laid out.

What do you think? Talk about the characters in a story. Which one do they like best? What's best about them? Is there a character they don't like?

Make connections. Where relevant, relate the story to your child's life, e.g. 'You do that sometimes, too, don't you?' or 'Would you like to do that, too?'.

Tell it again. Re-tell stories, without the book. You could even make up your own stories together. Invent different versions of familiar stories, e.g. 'One day Goldilocks went over to play with Baby Bear…'.

Act out a story together. Use dolls, teddies, puppets or other toys. Encourage your child to make up other stories. Then be their audience.

Shapes and sounds

Even before they start to recognise letters, young children discover that marks convey meaning, through everyday signs and symbols. Letters are the building blocks for reading words, so the first aim for your child is not only to recognise the **a-z** letter shapes, but to learn their sounds. So eyes and ears alert!

Alphabet Names

Teaching alphabet names **aee**, **bee**, **cee** etc. used to be the traditional starting point for learning **a-z**, but their names are not the same as letter sounds. For example, in the word **cat** the first letter name is **cee**, but its sound is a quiet **k…** sound. You will find that schools now start by teaching letter sounds first, not names, because the traditional letter names can be misleading. No less than 14 of them actually begin with another letter's sound! They are **f**, **l**, **m**, **n**, **s**, and **x** which all start with an **eh** sound, and **c(see)**, **g(jee)**, **h(aitch)**, **q(cue)**, **r(are)**, **u(you)**, **w(double-you)** and **y(why)**.

Alphabet Sounds

Current good practice means that children learn the letters of the alphabet in a much more 'natural' way, leaving alphabet name learning until they have a very clear understanding of the sounds that letters make, pronouncing each one exactly the way it sounds within regular words. This includes learning to just whisper the quiet sounds, such as **c**…, **fff**, **hhh**, **k**…, **p**…, **sss**, **t**… and **x**…(**ks**).

To support your child in pronouncing each sound correctly use the free online pronunciation guide (go to **www.letterland.com/parent-guide** and click on '2. Alphabet Sounds') and practise recognising all the **a-z** shapes as well. Don't worry if you don't have access to a computer to listen to the letter sounds online. You'll find these same tips for each letter on page 33 of this book. You can point to each one as you practise their sounds.

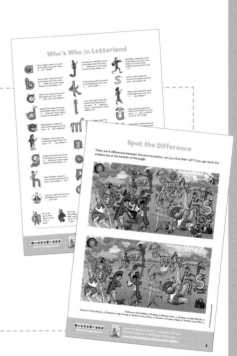

 Free downloads & resources

2. Alphabet Sounds
Use the online pronunciation guide with your child to practise the **a-z** sounds

3. Alphabet Activities
Downloadable spot the difference and colouring in activities.

4. Alphabet Songs
Listen online to a selection of the Letterland Alphabet Songs.

www.letterland.com/parent-guide

Letter formation

Most children start to enjoy making marks on paper and scribbling from the age of 2, 3 or 4 and like to pretend to 'write'. Soon they will want to write their name. This is the best time to make sure they form the letters correctly.

Getting the strokes right from the start is more valuable than it may first seem. Little children often develop poor hand habits, holding their pen or pencil awkwardly and, for example, making an **s** from the bottom up, writing **e**'s, **f**'s, **g**'s and **j**'s backwards and confusing **b**'s and **d**'s and **p**'s and **q**'s).

These awkward early hand grips and letter formation habits can be surprisingly hard to change. Unless caught early they can make it unnecessarily difficult to get rid of cramped writing, wrong letter formation, and letters written backwards. Later on, this can cause difficulty in learning joined-up writing. So, starting with the right hand grip and correct sequence of strokes can save many future frustrations.

Good hand positions for beginning writing

Left hander: Right hander:

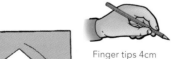

Finger tips 4cm
from tip of pencil

Paper side edge
30
Table edge

Elbows off the table

Finger tips 2cm
from tip of pencil

Paper side edge
20
Table edge

Chair slightly tilted

Free downloads & resources

5. Handwriting Songs
Listen online to a selection of the Letterland Handwriting Songs. See page 35 for the accompanying lyrics.

6. Finger Tracing
Watch the videos to learn how to finger trace.

7. Handwriting Practice
Practise forming a selection of the lowercase letters of the alphabet.

www.letterland.com/parent-guide

8. Draw the Letterlanders
Get creative, drawing the Letterlanders and see if they get featured on our artwork webpage!

9. Finger Puppets
A fun activity to help differentiate between the frequently confused letters **b** and **d**.

 Tips and activities for getting started

Just listen. Turn listening into a regular activity by finding moments to listen to sounds together – what can you hear in the house, in the street, in a shop, or walking to the park? Let your child tell you.

Signs and symbols. Talk about signs and symbols you see outside and what they mean (symbols for ladies and gents toilets, disabled parking spaces, green and red men at pedestrian crossings, road works signs). As they start to learn letter shapes, help them to spot them on signs, in shop names, product names, street names, etc. and capital letters on car licence plates.

Focus on shapes. Make a 'shape book' together. Your child could draw or trace common shapes (e.g. triangle, square, circle, rectangle, oval) and make patterns with them. You could then show how to write the words to label them. Find these basic shapes in the environment, too.

Label objects. Make labels together for objects and stick them around the house. You write the word, making the first letter hollow, and have your child colour it and place it by the object. Avoid words with two letter sounds (digraphs) like **ch** in **chair** at this stage while your focus is on just the **a-z** initial sounds.

Role play. Play games that involve writing, e.g. shops (list), doctors (note pad), cafes (menu and note pad), trips (tickets), schools (register, writing book).

Tips and activities for beginning writing

Model the letters. You could begin with playdough for fun. Make the letters and then add animating details in different colours.

Make an ABC scrapbook. Collect items that begin with each sound. Provide the correct spelling so they can model your writing to label the pictures.

Make display places. Show your child's pictures and writing on the on the fridge, in their bedrooms, or on a notice board, so they see that you value them.

Vary the tools. Give your child different things to write with on different days – a pen, coloured pencils, chalks or thick tipped markers. Add variety with a wet paint brush, or a stick to write with in sand. When you are in the kitchen you could give them a tray of flour, rice, lentils, or shaving cream to finger trace the letters in. You may also have access to a drawing app on a computer, tablet or smartphone – for practicing all those shapes.

Draw patterns. Show your child how to draw patterns, using different colours to make it fun. Zig zags, arches, straight lines and circles are all based on letter shapes, so they are good ways to start learning pencil control and letter formation.

Use old newspapers or magazines. Sit with your child while they look in headlines for letters they have just learned, and circle them with a red marker pen.

Independent writing. If your child does some writing on their own, ask them to read it to you and talk about what it says, even if you can't read a word of it. Correcting spelling mistakes can come later. Make sure they know you are impressed that they are having a go at capturing speech on paper. This really is impressive!

Use capital letters. As your child's writing gets more controlled and confident, you can encourage them to keep the letters on the line, and remind them about using capital letters for nam Letterland motivates correct use of capitals by explaining, for example, that Bouncy Ben is so pleased when he can start an important word, like a person's name or a new sentence, that he balances his blue ball between his big brown ears! And Harry Hat Man is so happy that he does a handstand at the start of important words!

Bouncy Ben loves to balance his best ball on his head whenever he is at the start of a name or a sentence.

When Harry Hat Man has the chance to start a name, he is so happy that he does a handstand. He still whispers his usual sound, '**hhh**...' and he even keeps his hat on!

Making words

Letter sounds

Once your child has learned a few letters and their sounds, they will be ready to read and then write some simple words! Knowing the correct letter sounds is essential (so don't be afraid to revisit the online pronunciation guide, or the one on page 33, if you want a quick refresher). Giving priority to letter sounds is also the reason that learning to read and write is often referred to as 'phonics' – which is just a more technical word for letter sounds.

Reading

Most schools now teach children to read using a process called 'blending'. This involves looking at a written word and speaking or 'sounding out' each letter's <u>sound</u> separately e.g. **h-a-t**. Extending or 'stretching' each sound can make this easier e.g. **hhh-aaa-t**. After making each sound separately, children are then taught to blend the sounds together, slowly at first and then quickly, until they can say the word smoothly as **hat**.

Writing

Writing down (or spelling) the words we speak simply reverses the blending process and is called 'segmenting'. In segmenting, each speech sound is said separately, e.g. **h-a-t**. Each sound may also be extended or stretched as it is spoken, e.g. **hhh-aaa-t**. This helps young children to correctly identify each sound in the word and then write its letter in the correct order, e.g. **hat**.

Since letters are a kind of code for the sounds we speak, it is worth noting that reading is sometimes also referred to as 'decoding' and writing (or spelling) as 'encoding'.

At the beginning, whether blending to read or segmenting to spell, children should start with short, simple words. These are often called CVC words because they start with a consonant, have a vowel in the middle and end with another consonant e.g. **cat**.

18

Although blending and segmenting may seem hard at first, the good thing about this approach is that children quickly learn that they can read and spell virtually all regular words without having to memorise them. This can really boost their confidence.

Once children are comfortable with reading and writing simple words they are ready to be introduced to longer, more complex words. Two letter sounds such as **sh**, **th**, **er** and **ow** are called 'digraphs' and need to be learned in order to read and spell words like <u>**shop**</u>, <u>**then**</u>, <u>**her**</u> and <u>**down**</u>. Three letter sounds such as **air** and **ear** are called 'trigraphs' and are needed for words like <u>**pair**</u> and <u>**hear**</u>. There is more information about digraphs and trigraphs in the downloads for the 'Reading to learn' section of this book and in the Letterland *Beyond ABC* and *Far Beyond ABC* books illustrated below.

Free downloads & resources

10. Blending Words
Use this download to give your child practice in the key skill of blending sounds smoothly together to read seven simple words.

11. Blends & Digraphs Songs
Listen online to a selection of the Letterland Blends & Digraph Songs.

12. Word Building Activity
Download and make your own flashcards and start building basic words with your child. See how many words you can make with only these letters: **s, m, t, p, a, e, o.**

www.letterland.com/parent-guide

 ## Tips for spelling

Letter sounds. Make sure that your child knows the correct sounds for all the letters that they have learned.

Sounding out. Encourage your child to slowly sound out and then write down simple words, saying each sound again while writing each letter. For example, say **swim**, then **sss-www-iii-mmm** and then **s-w-i-m**.

More words and little stories. When your child is ready, see if they would enjoy making little lists, writing their friends' names or even writing a one or two sentence story in a special note book.

Mistakes. At this early stage, don't worry if your child spells words the way they sound when spoken. For example, 'froot' for **fruit**, 'cofy' for **coffee** or 'jus' for **juice**. These sorts of 'mistakes' happen because English spellings are not always regular and your child has simply not learned them yet. But you can be encouraged that your child is still using their early phonic knowledge and will soon learn to deal with these more difficult spellings.

Dictionaries. You could also buy a starter picture dictionary or help your child to learn to use a larger dictionary – paper or online – if you need to check a spelling or the meaning of a new word.

Common irregular words. Once your child can sound out regular words with confidence, you could start supporting them in learning to read and spell some of the 100 most common high frequency words. These are listed on page 37. It is a good idea to explain that some of these words are tricky and are trying to catch us out! Do encourage your child to sound out the regular parts of the words, as this will help your child to use their phonic skills as much as they can. You might even have a bet with them to see if they can remember the other parts! If your child becomes discouraged, just turn to something that they can do well, so that their confidence is built up.

 Tips for beginner readers

Success. Remember that success is important to keep your child motivated and happy. Only ask them to read words or stories that you know they will be able to read. Books that are just made up of words that your child can read are called 'decodable books'. Decodable books that are at the right level for your child should be available through their school or from public libraries. Their drawback, however, is that they are not always very interesting. So, do continue to read as wide a range of books to your child as you can.

Finger pointing. In the early stages, use your finger to point to words as you read them. Encourage your child to do the same as they sound out easy words. That little index finger on the page helps them to keep focused and keeps their eyes moving in the reading direction.

Stuck? If your child is stuck on a word, give them a little time to try working it out, but also feel free to sound it out for them or just say it. Remember that the aim is to get your child reading for meaning, and enjoying it.

Story first. When you know the next word will be difficult, avoid frustration by providing it without waiting, so you can get on with the story.

Take turns. Take it in turns to read a sentence or page of their reading book from school. Some children may find a lot of text quite off-putting or tiring, even if they can read it. Remember, your long term aim is for your child not just to learn to read, but to enjoy books so that reading becomes a lifelong habit!

Share the support.
Share the supporting role of your young reader with as many family members and friends as possible. Fathers, uncles, grandparents, teenagers – their interest and attention can tip the balance, for boys and girls alike, into becoming a reader for life.

Get the meaning. Often in the early stages children can't easily decode words and follow the story as well. So it is a good idea, from time to time, to reread a sentence or two out loud together after your child has successfully sounded the words out, to make sure they can still enjoy the story.

Just enjoy. During the stage when your child is still reading slowly and with some effort, make sure you also take time to enjoy just reading to them.

Be a cheerleader. Encourage your child when they are reading and writing, at whatever level, and show them you are proud of their new skill.

Praise words. Have fun yourself thinking of as many ways as you can to give praise, e.g. admirable, brilliant, clever, correct, well done, excellent, good effort, fabulous, good going, hurrah, you did it without any help!, etc. All are little ways you can vary your praise, while also broadening your child's vocabulary.

Go hunting. Go on a 'Letter Hunt' or a 'Word Hunt'. Make a game of spotting and counting the number of times one of the 100 most common high frequency words (see page 37 for a full list) in the English language turns up in a story or a page of a newspaper. Later you could do a hunt with particular spelling patterns your child has just been learning, such as **ay** or **a-e**, **oi**, etc.

Many teachers send books or other reading material home. Make sure your child reads these with you. You can take turns doing the reading, but if your child's reading is slow and halting, it is a good idea to have them reread all, or parts of the story, again. You can help by first reading one paragraph or one page to them, and then have them reread it. Alternatively, you could both read it aloud at the same time. Check with your child's teacher about their progress in reading and ask how you can best support their learning at home.

Swap roles. After school, sometimes ask your child if they learned something new today that they can teach you. Swapping roles (so you are not the one who is always handing out the information) can work well in a variety of situations.

 ## Tips for more confident readers

As your child becomes more confident in their reading it is still important to always have good books on hand so you can share stories with them, explain new words and phrases, and help them to further expand their vocabularies. As your child's concentration span gets longer, you can read and discuss more complex books, such as short chapter books or longer stories.

Rhymes. Read books together that have nonsense or rhyming words in them. In particular, books by Roald Dahl or Dr Seuss are especially good.

Use the Internet. Check out www.booktrust.org.uk. It has an excellent 'Bookfinder' tool linked to age. Parents in the USA will find www.reading.org useful, including the Children's Choices section, listing books chosen by young readers.

Audiobooks. Include books with an audio CD, so your child can listen to them when you can be nearby but are otherwise busy. There are some very fine recordings of classical tales that all children love.

Books galore. Swap children's books with friends. Buy books as birthday presents. Borrow library books as often as you can.

Laugh together. Enjoy joke and pun books together that 'play' with words.

Read the environment. Spot letters and words on signs, etc. that are written in different fonts and talk about why. Perhaps it is for emphasis, to catch your eye, or to make it look handwritten and more personal.

Signs and symbols. Talk about punctuation in stories. See how different sentences sound when you read them with or without particular punctuation marks, such as ?, !, commas and quotation marks. Make sure they know the meaning of these signs: &, @, £, €,and $.

Crosswords. Do crosswords with your child. You can work out the clues together and they can fill in the words.

Explain new words. If you are reading a longer book, don't worry if some of the wording seems a bit too advanced. Many will be good opportunities to explain new words, once again helping to broaden your child's vocabulary.

Be authors. Make up a story together by taking a line each, e.g.

Parent: 'Once upon a time there was a butterfly with only one wing.' Child: 'One day he decided to go to the shop to buy another one,' and so on.

Look around. Scour the environment at a new level. For example, when your child is learning at school about 'split digraphs' (also known as 'silent Magic **e** words'), look out together for more words of the same structure, like **sale**, **price** and **size** in the shops, on street names with **Close**, **Drive**, **Grove** and **Place**, and on household words like **flakes**, **volume** and **tone**.

Electronic Books. Read eBooks or stories on-screen together so your child gets used to hearing and seeing stories in different formats.

Reading to learn

Becoming a fluent reader means being able to read words so effortlessly that your child is free to give full attention to the meaning in every sentence and to read with expression. This is the important stage of moving on from learning to read to the ultimate goal – reading for enjoyment! This is the life skill we all want for our children so that they become learners for life.

Fluency is the ability to read a text quickly, accurately, and with proper expression. Comprehension is about actively seeking out and understanding the meaning of the text. In fact, reading with expression only works when your child fully understands the message in each sentence and paragraph. An important way to help develop fluency and comprehension is through rereading.

Aiming for fluency

Some children seem to read words fluently but have little understanding of the story. Although they may seem fluent, in fact they may be concentrating so much on decoding the words that it is difficult for them to focus on the meaning of whole sentences at the same time.

If so, they may need to spend more time in mastering the sounds made by two letter and three letter spelling patterns like **ar**, **ew**, **oa**, **igh**, etc. to broaden the number of words they can read without hesitation. With each one they learn well, hundreds of words containing that same spelling pattern will become easy to read. So the more sounds your child knows well, the fewer words there will be to stumble over and the easier it will be to focus on what the words mean.

car new goal light

⬇ Free downloads & resources

13. Spelling Patterns
Letterland uses engaging stories to explain what happens when letters come together to make new sounds in words (digraphs). Your child will quickly discover how easy it is to remember the new sound just by learning the story.

Play the videos which animate a selection of sample stories and have fun finding illustrated objects that contain the new sound. You can also download the stories as a PDF to read in your own time.

www.letterland.com/parent-guide

Tips for fluency and comprehension

Model fluent reading. When your child reads to you, help them to read with 'flow' and expression by taking turns. You read a sentence with expression. They copy your voice and go on to the next sentence, ideally still keeping up the expressive tone of voice. Change your voices when characters speak, or lower them when a story gets scary. This will not only give your child practice in reading fluently, but will also bring the story to life.

Read it again. Reread favourite stories and poems together, with your child focusing on using their voice to make the reading sound interesting for others to hear. Take turns to keep it light-hearted.

Focus on meaning. Practise by asking your child to get ready to answer one or two questions you will ask them after they reread a section to you. Give questions about what's happening, or what they think might happen next. Help them with suggestions like, 'Could you say that...?'.

Focus on text. As your child becomes more confident with their reading and writing, you can read longer and more exciting stories together. You can also talk about details of the text, for example, to notice different endings on verbs, to obey punctuation marks of all kinds. Missing a comma can completely change a sentence's meaning! So accuracy is important for both fluency and comprehension.

Focus on the author. Draw your child's attention to the person behind the words they are reading. What was he or she saying? Have we understood their message? Good readers think all the time as they read.

Wonder together. Take a problem or event in the story and wonder out loud together, 'What would you do if...?' 'Do you think the author wanted to surprise you with the way the story ended?' Do interrupt the story to answer any question your child may ask.

Motivate. Make sure to have good books on hand that they will want to read so they continue to get better at reading simply by doing more of it! The more they read independently, the more they are experiencing firsthand how many places they can 'go' and things they can 'do' – just by getting absorbed in a book – and what a useful and enjoyable skill reading actually is!

Common problems

When should I start reading with my child?
It is never too early to introduce your child to books. Babies and toddlers love looking at picture books and hearing you read aloud. You can share books from birth onwards!

When is the best time to read with my child?
When nothing is competing for their time. If you choose good books and really enjoy them together, so that your child is actually preferring a cosy read with you, you are winning!

Should I teach my child the alphabet before they start school?
Parents often think teaching the letter names, **aee**, **bee**, **cee**, etc. will give them a head start before school. In fact only 5 letter names (**a**, **e**, **i**, **o**, **u**) are ever used in reading! So this is not the best time to emphasise alphabet names. But do get your child interested in letter shapes and their sounds. To make sure you are teaching the sounds correctly, see the Shapes and Sounds section, page 11.

My child wants me to read the same book over and over again. Surely we should be reading other things by now?
Young children often ask for the same again and again. This can be very frustrating, especially since they seem to have a knack of loving the book you like the least! However, rereading familiar stories gives them confidence and there is obviously something in the book that has captured their imagination. Give them other new book choices and eventually they will move on and find another favourite.

My child is a confident reader, but still wants me to read to her books written for younger children.
As children grow older and become more independent and skillful, they still like to return to things they remember from younger days – books, toys or television programmes, for example. It might be that reading simpler books gives them happy or secure memories of being younger and more dependent, or that they feel more secure reading a book that they know they won't struggle with. Reading easy books, both to and with them is still useful, but you might want to combine them with longer, more challenging stories where you take turns, with your turns longer than theirs.

My child is on a lower level reading book than the rest of the class.
Children develop in different ways and at different speeds. Literacy is a complex skill involving many developmental abilities, and children of the same age in the same class will be at completely different stages of literacy development. In addition, a reading scheme may have different sub-levels within a reading level,

which will have their own numbering scheme and be difficult to compare. What is more important is whether your child enjoys reading and can talk about the story. If you think your child's reading book needs changing, or you'd like to give more informed help, speak to their class teacher. However, try not to compare levels with other children in the class as reading schemes are not designed to be a race!

Should I correct my child's spelling?

In the early days of writing your child is unlikely to get every word right. They may also spell purely phonetically e.g. 'froot' for **fruit** or 'berd' for **bird**. Encourage and praise them for what they are saying on paper, rather than pointing out wrong spellings. Too much correcting can discourage them and put them off writing.

What do I do if my child gets stuck reading a word?

In the early stages, just say the word for them, especially if it is a difficult one. For easier words, you may want to give them enough time to try sounding it out before jumping in, or just sound out the irregular part for them. On balance, if there is a risk that their stumbling will destroy their interest in reading, quickly give them the word.

My child writes certain letters back to front like b, d, p, q. What should I do?

It is very common for children, especially in the early days of learning to write, to get letters the wrong way round. (For help see page 13).

I'm not a very confident reader and my spelling is poor. How can I help my child have confidence in their reading and writing?

The most important thing you can do is encourage and praise your child when they read to you or do some writing, and support them in their learning. You could even share with them that you never became a good reader, so they may well be able to teach you some things they learn at school that you didn't know. Some schools or local education centres also run classes to help adults with their literacy skills. Joining one will show your child that learning is good for grown-ups too.

English isn't my first language. Which language should I use to talk to my child about books?

Use which ever language you feel most comfortable speaking. It doesn't matter which language you use, you are still talking about books and enjoying them together. If you prefer, read books in your own language as well. You can also get an increasing number of picture books in dual language versions from libraries and bookshops.

 Free downloads & resources

14. Common problems
Find more answers to common problems relating to reading and writing.

www.letterland.com/parent-guide

Who's who in Letterland

Letter sounds

Annie Apple makes the sound at the beginning of her name – 'ă…' (as in ăpple).

Bouncy Ben makes the sound at the beginning of his name – 'b…'. Keep your mouth nearly closed to avoid adding "uh".

Clever Cat makes the sound at the beginning of her name – 'c…' (as in cat). Just whisper it.

Dippy Duck makes the sound at the beginning of her name – 'd…'. Keep your mouth nearly closed to avoid adding "uh".

Eddy Elephant makes the sound at the beginning of his name – 'ĕ…' (as in ĕlephant).

Firefighter Fred makes the sound at the beginning of his name – 'fff…'. Just whisper it.

Golden Girl makes the sound at the beginning of her name – 'g…'. Keep your mouth nearly closed to avoid adding "uh".

Harry Hat Man makes the sound at the beginning of his name. Just whisper it – 'hhh…'.

Impy Ink makes the sound at the beginning of his name – 'ĭ…' (as in ĭnk).

Jumping Jim makes the sound at the beginning of his name – 'j…'. Keep your mouth nearly closed to avoid adding "uh".

Kicking King makes the sound at the beginning of his name – 'k…'. Just whisper it.

Lucy Lamp Light makes the sound at the beginning of her name – 'lll…'. Keep your mouth nearly closed to avoid adding "uh".

Munching Mike makes the sound at the beginning of his name. Keep your mouth closed and hum 'mmm…' to avoid adding "uh".

Noisy Nick makes the sound at the beginning of his name. Keep your mouth nearly closed and lips open – 'nnn…' to avoid adding "uh".

Oscar Orange makes the sound at the beginning of his name – 'ŏ…' (as in ŏrange).

Peter Puppy makes the sound at the beginning of his name – '**p**...'. Just whisper it.

Quarrelsome Queen makes the sound at the beginning of her name – '**qu**...'. Whisper "**kw**".

Red Robot makes the sound at the beginning of his name. Keep your mouth nearly closed and prolong his sound – '**rrr**...'.

Sammy Snake makes the sound at the beginning of his name. Just whisper '**sss**...'.

Talking Tess makes the sound at the beginning of her name – '**t**...'. Just whisper it.

Uppy Umbrella makes the sound at the beginning of her name – 'ŭ...' (as in ŭmbrella). For once "uh" is right!

Vicky Violet makes the sound at the beginning of her name – '**vvv**...'. Keep your mouth nearly closed to avoid adding "uh".

Walter Walrus makes the sound at the beginning of his name. Get ready to whistle but blow instead – '**www**...'. Try not to add "uh".

Fix-it Max makes the last sound in his name. He makes the sound '**ks**...' in words. Just whisper it.

Yellow Yo-yo Man makes the sound at the beginning of his name. Keep your mouth nearly closed – '**yyy**...' to avoid adding "uh".

Zig Zag Zebra makes the sound at the beginning of her name – '**zzz**...'. Keep your mouth nearly closed to avoid adding "uh".

The Vowel Men

The only men that ever say their traditional alphabet names in words are the five Vowel Men, Mr A, Mr E, Mr I, Mr O, and Mr U.

Mr A, the Apron Man, says his name '**A**' as in **a**pron.

Mr E, the Easy Magic Man, says his name '**E**' as in **e**asy.

Mr I, the Ice Cream Man, says his name '**I**' as in **i**ce cream.

Mr O, the Old Man from over the Ocean, says his name '**O**' as in **o**ld.

Mr U, the Uniform Man, says his name '**U**' as in **u**niform.

Alphabet Songs

Introduce your child to the Letterland characters and the sounds they make with 26 lively songs sung to well-known nursery tunes.

Who's who in Letterland

Letter shapes

Annie Apple
At the leaf begin.
Go round the apple this way.
Then add a line down,
so Annie won't roll away.

Bouncy Ben
Brush down Ben's
big, long ears.
Go up and round his head
so his face appears!

Clever Cat
Curve round Clever Cat's
face to begin.
Then gently tickle her
under her chin.

Dippy Duck
Draw Dippy Duck's back.
Go round her tum.
Go up to her head.
Then down you come!

Eddy Elephant
Ed has a headband.
Draw it and then
stroke round his head
and his trunk to the end.

Firefighter Fred
First draw Fred's helmet.
Then go down a way.
Give him some arms
and he'll put out the blaze.

Golden Girl
Go round Golden Girl's head.
Go down her golden hair.
Then curve to make her swing,
so she can sit there.

Harry Hat Man
Hurry from the Hat Man's head
down to his heel on the ground.
Go up and bend his knee over.
so he'll hop while he makes
his sound.

Impy Ink
Inside the ink bottle
draw a line.
Add an inky dot.
That's fine!

Jumping Jim
Just draw down Jim,
bending his knees.
Then add the one ball
which everyone sees.

Kicking King
Kicking King's body
is a straight stick.
Add his arm,
then his leg,
so he can kick!

Lucy Lamp Light
Lucy looks like one long line.
Go straight from head to foot
and she's ready to shine!

Munching Mike
Make Munching Mike's
back leg first,
then his second leg, and third,
so he can go
munch-munching in a word.

Noisy Nick
'Now bang my nail,'
Noisy Nick said.
'Go up and over
around my head.'

Oscar Orange
On Oscar Orange
start at the top.
Go all the way round him,
and... then stop.

Peter Puppy
Pat Peter Puppy properly.
First stroke down his ear,
then up and round his face
so he won't shed a tear.

Quarrelsome Queen
Quickly go round the
Queen's cross face.
Then comb her beautiful
hair into place.

Red Robot
Run down Red Robot's body.
Go up to his arm and his hand.
Then watch out for this robot
roaming round Letterland.

Sammy Snake
Start at Sam's head
where he can see.
Stroke down to his tail,
oh so care-ful-ly!

Talking Tess
Tall as a tower make
Talking Tess stand.
Go from head to toe,
and then from hand to hand.

Uppy Umbrella
Under the umbrella
draw a shape like a cup.
Then draw a straight line
so it won't tip up.

Vicky Violet
Very neatly,
start at the top.
Draw down your vase,
then up and stop.

Walter Walrus
When you draw the
Walrus' wells,
with wild and wavy water,
whizz down and up
and then...,
whizz down and up again.

Fix-it Max
Fix two sticks,
to look like this.
That's how to draw
a little kiss.

Yellow Yo-yo Man
You first make the yo-yo sack
on the Yo-yo Man's back,
and then go down to his toes
so he can sell his yo-yos.

Zig Zag Zebra
Zip along Zig Zag's nose.
Stroke her neck...,
stroke her back...
Zzzoom! Away she goes.

Handwriting Songs
You can listen to all of these verses on the popular **Handwriting Songs** CD, a highly effective way to learn correct letter shape formation.

100 high frequency words

1. the
2. and
3. a
4. to
5. said
6. in
7. he
8. I
9. of
10. it
11. was
12. you
13. they
14. on
15. she
16. is
17. for
18. at
19. his
20. but
21. that
22. with
23. all
24. we
25. can
26. are
27. up

28. had
29. my
30. her
31. what
32. there
33. out
34. this
35. have
36. went
37. be
38. like
39. some
40. so
41. not
42. then
43. were
44. go
45. little
46. as
47. no
48. mum
49. one
50. them
51. do
52. me
53. down
54. dad

55. big		**78.** their
56. when		**79.** people
57. it's		**80.** your
58. see		**81.** put
59. looked		**82.** could
60. very		**83.** house
61. look		**84.** old
62. don't		**85.** too
63. come		**86.** by
64. will		**87.** day
65. into		**88.** made
66. back		**89.** time
67. from		**90.** I'm
68. children		**91.** if
69. him		**92.** help
70. Mr		**93.** Mrs
71. get		**94.** called
72. just		**95.** here
73. now		**96.** off
74. came		**97.** asked
75. oh		**98.** saw
76. about		**99.** make
77. got		**100.** an

 Free downloads

15. High frequency words
Download a list of the 100 most common high frequency words that includes a helpful key to regular and irregular spelling patterns and guidance on the trickiest words to focus on.

www.letterland.com/parent-guide

Glossary

Blend: when children have learned individual letter sounds, they blend – put them together – to form whole words, e.g. **rrr-u-nnn**, **run**.

CVC words: Simple words containing a consonant, a vowel, and another consonant, in that order, e.g. **pot**, **mat**, **cat**, **cut**. Children typically learn CVC words as the first step in learning to decode (sound out) the letters to turn them into meaningful words.

Decodable words: Words a reader can sound out, because he or she has been taught all the phonic facts that occur in those particular words.

Digraph: two letters together that represent one sound e.g. **ph**, **ch**, **gh** (consonant digraphs) or **ai**, **ea**, **oo**, **au** (vowel digraphs).

Fluency: the ability to read a text quickly, accurately, and with proper expression and understanding.

Comprehension: the ability to understand the messages in print at various levels, and well enough to read them with expression.

High frequency words: common words that occur most frequently in writing, e.g. **and**, **the**, **as**, **it**. Children are expected to recognize different high frequency words depending on which year they are in at school.

Phonics: knowledge of the speech sounds that letters make in words, not their names, so for **cat**, not **see ay tee** but the sounds **c**... **a**... **t**.

Regular words: All words that a child can read by just using their first knowledge of the 26 **a-z** sounds.

Segment: breaking a word into its individual letter sounds, e.g. **cat**, **c**... **a**... **t**.

Sight vocabulary: words that children learn to recognize at a glance by their overall look, rather than by sounding out each letter.

Synthetic phonics: a description of the method of learning to read whereby children learn letter sounds and how to blend these sounds together to make words.

Trigraph: three letters together that represent one unit of sound e.g. **igh**.

⬇ Free downloads & resources

Introduction to Letterland
1. Introduction to Letterland

Alphabet sounds
🎵 2. Alphabet Sounds
🎵 3. Alphabet Activities
🎵 4. Alphabet Songs

Letter formation
🎵 5. Handwriting Songs
6. Finger Tracing
7. Handwriting Practice
8. Draw the Letterlanders
9. Finger Puppets

Spelling
10. Blending Words
🎵 11. Blends & Digraphs Songs
12. Word Building Activity

Aiming for fluency
13. Spelling Patterns

Useful resources
14. Common Problems
15. 100 High Frequency Words List
16. Glossary

www.letterland.com/parent-guide

Letterland

Child-friendly phonics

The Letterland system teaches all 44 sounds in the English language through stories rather than rules. There are resources to take children from the very first stages of learning to full literacy.

ABC Trilogy

Handwriting Practice

Activity Book Sets

Picture Books

Sticker Activity Books

Games & puzzles

See our full range at: **www.letterland.com**
For product advice and support: **info@letterland.com**